I0015992

Microsoft Word 2016
Keyboard Shortcuts

For Windows

By

U. C-Abel Books.

All Rights Reserved

First Edition: 2016

Copyright @ U. C-Abel Books. ISBN-13:978-1533598806

This book, Microsoft Word 2016 Keyboard Shortcuts For Windows has been licensed by copyright proprietors, therefore reproducing it in any way including creating an alternative format without a prior written permission from the copyright holder is an infringement of copyright and violators will be punished. However, it can be used in the case of brief quotations in critical articles or reviews.

ISBN-13:978-1533598806
ISBN-10: 1533598800

Published by U. C-Abel Books.

Table of Contents

Acknowledgement.

U. C-Abel Books will not take all the credits for Microsoft Word 2016 keyboard shortcuts listed in this book, but shares it with Microsoft Corporation because some of the shortcut keys came from them and are "used with permission from Microsoft".

Dedication

This book is dedicated to computer users and lovers of keyboard shortcuts all over the world.

Introduction.

We enjoy using shortcut keys because they set us on a high plane that astonishes people around us when we work with them. As wonderful shortcuts users, the worst eyesore we witness in computing is to see somebody sluggishly struggling to execute a task through mouse usage when in actual sense shortcuts will help to save that person the time wasted. Most people have asked us to help them with a list of shortcut keys that can make them work as smartly as we do and that drove us into research to broaden our knowledge and truly help them as they demanded, that is the reason for the existence of this book. It is a great tool for lovers of shortcuts, and those who want to join the group.

Most times, the things we love don't come by easily. It is our love for keyboard shortcuts that made us to bear long sleepless nights like owls, just to make sure we get the best out of it, and it is the best we got that we are sharing with you in this book. You cannot be the same at computing after reading this book. The time you entrusted to our care is an expensive possession and we promise not to mess it up.

Thank you.

What to Know Before You Begin.

General Notes.

1. It is important to note that when using shortcuts to perform any command, you should make sure the target area is active, if not, you may get a wrong result. Example, if you want to highlight all texts, you must make sure the text field is active and if an object, make sure the object area is active. The active area is always known by the location where the cursor of your computer blinks.

2. Most of the keyboard shortcuts you will see in this book refer to the U.S. keyboard layout. Keys for other layouts might not correspond exactly to the keys on a U.S. keyboard.

3. The plus (+) signs that come in the middle of keyboard shortcuts simply mean the keys are meant to be combined or held down together not to be added as one of the shortcut keys. In a case where plus sign is needed; it will be duplicated (++).

4. For keyboard shortcuts in which you press one key immediately followed by another key, the keys are separated by a comma (,).

5. It is also important to note that the shortcut keys listed in this book are for Microsoft Word 2016.

Short Forms Used in This Book and Their Full Meaning.

The following are short forms of keyboard shortcuts used in this Microsoft Word 2016 Keyboard Shortcuts book and their full meaning.

1. Alt   -   Alternate Key
2. Caps Lock   -   Caps Lock Key
3. Ctrl   -   Control Key
4. Esc   -   Escape Key
5. F   -   Function Key
6. Num Lock   -   Number Lock Key
7. Shft   -   Shift Key
8. Tab   -   Tabulate Key
9. Win   -   Windows logo key
10. Prt sc   -   Print Screen

CHAPTER 1.

Gathering The Basic Knowledge Of Keyboard Shortcuts.

Without the existence of the keyboard, there wouldn't have been anything like keyboard shortcuts, so in this chapter we will learn a little about keyboard before moving to keyboard shortcuts.

1. Definition of Computer Keyboard.

This is an input device that is used to send data to the computer memory.

Sketch of a Keyboard

1.1 Types of Keyboard.

i. Standard (Basic) Keyboard.
ii. Enhanced (Extended) Keyboard.

i. **Standard Keyboard:** This is a keyboard designed during the 1800s for mechanical typewriters with just 10 function keys (F keys) placed at the left side of it.

ii. **Enhanced Keyboard:** This is the current 101 to 102-key keyboard that is included in almost all the personal computers (PCs) of nowadays, which has 12 function keys at the top side of it.

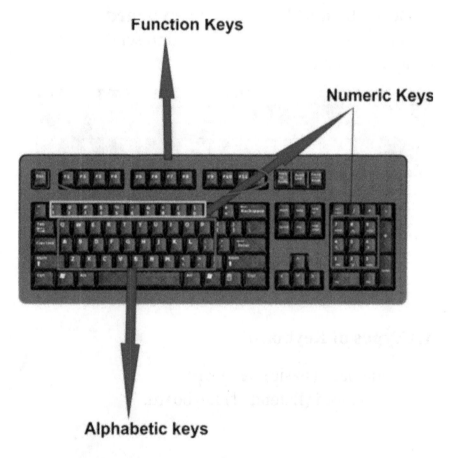

Function Keys

Numeric Keys

Alphabetic keys

1.2 Segments of the keyboard

- Numeric keys
- Alphabetic keys
- Punctuation keys
- Windows Logo key.
- Function keys
- Special keys

Numeric Keys: Numeric keys are keys with numbers from **0 - 9**.

Alphabetic Keys: These are keys that have alphabets on them, ranging from **A-Z**.

Punctuation Keys: These are keys of the keyboard used for punctuation. Examples include comma, full stop, colon, question marks, hyphen etc.

Windows Logo Key: A key on Microsoft Computer keyboard with its logo displayed on it. Search for this ⊞ on your keyboard.

Function Keys: These are keys that have **F** on them which are usually combined with other keys. They are F1 - F12, and are also in the class called Special Keys.

Special Keys: These are keys that perform special functions. They include: Tab, Ctrl, Caps lock, Insert,

Prt sc, alt gr, Shift, Home, Num lock, Esc and many others. Special keys work according to the type of computer involved. In some keyboard layout, especially laptops, the keys that turn the speaker on/off, the one that increases/decreases volume, the key that turns the computer Wifi on/off are also special keys.

Other Special Keys Worthy of Note.

Enter Key: This is located at the right-hand corner of the keyboard. It is used to send messages to the computer to execute commands, in most cases it is used to mean "Ok" or "Go".

Escape Key (ESC): This is the first key on the upper left of the keyboard. It is used to cancel routines, close menus and select options such as **Save** according to circumstance.

Control Key (CTRL): It is located on the bottom row of the left and right hand side of the keyboard. They also work with the function keys to execute commands using Keyboard shortcuts (key combinations).

Alternate Key (ALT): It is located on the bottom row, very close to the CTRL key on both side of the keyboard. It enables many editing functions to be accomplished by using some keystroke combinations on the keyboard.

Shift Key: This adds to the functions of the function keys. In addition, it enables the use of alternative function of a particular button (key), especially, those with more than one function on a key. E.g. use of capital letters, symbols and numbers.

1.3. Selecting/Highlighting With the Keyboard.

This is a highlighting method or style where data is selected using the keyboard instead of a computer mouse.

To do this:

- Move your cursor to the text you want to highlight, make sure that area is active,
- Hold down the shift key with one finger
- Then use another finger to move the arrow key that points to the direction you want to highlight.

1.4 The Operating Modes Of The Keyboard.

Just like the mouse the keyboard has two operating modes. The two modes are Text Entering and Command Mode.

a. **Text Entering Mode:** this mode gives the operator/user the opportunity to type text.

b.　**Command Mode:** this is used to command the operating system/software/application to execute commands in certain ways.

2. Ways To Improve In Your Typing Skill.

1. Put Your Eyes Off The Keyboard.

This is the aspect of keyboard usage that many don't find funny because they always ask. "How can I put my eyes off the keyboard when I am running away from the occurrence of errors on my file?" My aim is to be fast, is this not going to slow me down?

Of course, there will be errors and at the same time your speed will slow down but the motive behind the introduction of this method is to make you faster than you are. Looking at your keyboard while you type can make you get a sore neck, it is better you learn to touch type because the more you type with your eyes fixed on the screen instead of the keyboard, the faster you become.
An alternative to keeping your eyes off your keyboard is to use the "*Das Keyboard Ultimate*".

2. Errors Challenge You
It is better to fail than not to try at all. Not trying at all is an attribute of the weak and lazybones. When you

make mistakes, try again because errors are opportunities for improvement.

3. Good Posture (Position Yourself Well).
Do not adopt an awkward position while typing. You should get everything on your desk organized or arranged before sitting to type. Your posture while typing contributes to your speed and productivity.

4. Practice
Here is the conclusion of everything said above. You have to practice your shortcuts constantly. The practice alone is a way of improvement. "Practice brings improvement". Practice always.

2.1 Software That Will Help You Improve In Your Typing Skill.

There are several Software programs for typing that both kids and adults can use for their typing skill. Here is a list of software that can help you improve in your typing: Mavis Beacon, Typing Instructor, Mucky Typing Adventure, Rapid Tying Tutor, Letter Chase Tying Tutor, Alice Touch Typing Tutor and many more. Personally, I recommend Mavis Beacon.

To learn typing with MAVIS BEACON, install Mavis Beacon software to your computer, start with keyboard lesson, then move to games. Games like **Penguin Crossing, Creature Lab** or **Space Junk** will help you become a professional in typing. Typing and keyboard shortcuts work hand-in-hand.

Sketch of a computer mouse

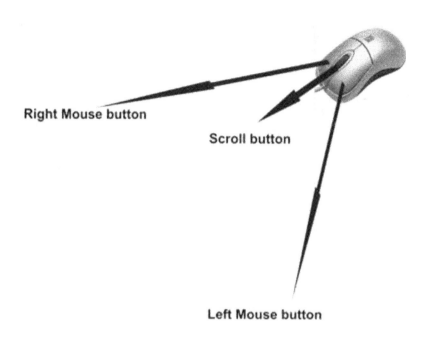

Right Mouse button

Scroll button

Left Mouse button

3. Mouse:

This is an oval-shaped portable input device with three buttons for scrolling, left clicking, and right clicking that enables work to be done effectively on a computer. The plural form of mouse is mice.

3.1 Types of Computer Mouse

- Mechanical Mouse
- Optical Mechanical Mouse (Optomechanical)
- Laser Mouse
- Optical Mouse

- BlueTrack Mouse

3.2 Forms of Clicking:

Left Clicking: This is the process of clicking the left side button of the mouse. It can be called *clicking* without the addition of *left*.

Right Clicking: It is the process of clicking the right side button of the mouse.

Double Clicking: It is the process of clicking the left side button two times (twice) and immediately.

Double clicking is used to select a word while thrice clicking is used to select a sentence or paragraph.

Scroll Button: It is the little key attached to the mouse that looks like a tiny wheel. It takes you up and down a page when moved.

3.3 Mouse Pad: This is a small soft mat that is placed under the mouse to make it have a free movement.

3.4 Laptop Mouse Touchpad

This unlike the mouse we explained above is not external, rather it is inbuilt (comes with a laptop computer). With the presence of a laptop mouse touchpad, an external mouse is not needed to use a laptop, except in a case where it is malfunctioning or the operator prefers to use external one for some reasons.

The laptop mouse touchpad is usually positioned at the end of the keyboard section of a laptop computer. It is rectangular in shape with two buttons positioned below it. The two buttons/keys are used for left and right clicking just like the external mouse. Some laptops come with four mouse keys. Two placed above the mouse for left and right clicking and two other keys placed below it for the same function.

4. Definition Of Keyboard Shortcuts.

Keyboard shortcuts are defined as a series of keys, sometimes with combination that execute tasks that typically involve the use of mouse or other input devices.

5. Why You Should Use Shortcuts.

1. One may not be able to use a computer mouse easily because of disability or pain.

2. One may not be able to see the mouse pointer as a result of vision impairment, in such case what will the person do? The answer is SHORTCUT.

3. Research has made it known that Extensive mouse usage is related to Repetitive Syndrome Injury (RSI) greatly than the use of keyboard.

4. Keyboard shortcuts speed up computer users, making learning them a worthwhile effort.

5. When performing a job that requires precision, it is wise that you use the keyboard instead of mouse, for instance, if you are dealing with Text Editing, it is better you handle it using keyboard shortcuts than spending more time with mouse alone.

6. Studies calculate that using keyboard shortcuts allows working 10 times faster than working with the mouse. The time you spend looking for the mouse and then getting the cursor to the position you want is lost! Reducing your work duration by 10 times brings you greater results.

5.1 Ways To Become A Lover Of Shortcuts.

1. Always have the urge to learn new shortcut keys associated with the programs you use.
2. Be happy whenever you learn a new shortcut.
3. Try as much as you can to apply the new shortcuts you learnt.
4. Always bear it in mind that learning new shortcuts is worth it.

5. Always remember that the use of keyboard shortcuts keeps people healthy while performing computing activities.

5.2 How To Learn New Shortcut Keys

1. Do a research for them: quick reference (a cheat sheet comprehensively compiled) can go a long way to help you improve.
2. Buy applications that show you keyboard shortcuts every time you execute an action with the mouse.
3. Disconnect your mouse if you must learn this fast.
4. Read user manuals and help topics (Whether offline or online).

5.3 Your Reward For Knowing Shortcut Keys.

1. You will get faster unimaginably.
2. Your level of efficiency will increase.
3. You will find it easy to use.
4. Opportunities are high that you will become an expert in what you do.
5. You won't have to go for **Office button**, click **New,** click **Blank and Recent** and click **Create** just to insert a fresh/blank page. **Ctrl +N** takes care of that in a second.

A Funny Note: Keyboard Shortcuts and Mousing are in a marital union with Keyboard Shortcuts being the head and it will be unfair for anybody to put asunder between them.

5.4 Why We Emphasize On The Use of Shortcuts.

You may never ditch your mouse completely unless you are ready to make your brain a box of keyboard shortcuts which will really be frustrating. Just imagine yourself learning all the shortcuts for the programs you use and its various versions. You shouldn't learn keyboard shortcuts that way.

Why we are emphasizing on the use of shortcuts is because mouse usage is becoming unusually common and unhealthy, too. So we just want to make sure both are combined so you can get fast, productive and healthy in your computing activities. All you need to know is just the most important ones associated with the programs you use.

CHAPTER 2.

15 (Fifteen) Special Keyboard Shortcuts.

The fifteen special keyboard shortcuts are fifteen (15) shortcut keys every computer user should know.

The following table contains the list of keyboard shortcuts every computer user should know.

1. **Ctrl + A:** Control plus A, highlights or selects everything you have in the environment where you are working.

> *If you are like **"Wow, the content of this document is large and there is no time to select all of it, besides, it's going to mount pressure on my computer?"** Using the mouse for this is an outdated method of handling a task like selecting all, Ctrl+A will take care of that within seconds.*

2. **Ctrl + C:** Control plus C copies any highlighted or selected element within the work environment.

> *Saves the time and stress which would have been used to right click and click again just to copy. Use ctrl+c.*

3. **Ctrl + N:** Control plus N opens a new window. *Instead of clicking* **File, New, blank/ template** *and another* **click***, just press* ***Ctrl + N*** *and a fresh window will appear instantly.*

4. **Ctrl + O:** Control plus O opens a new program. *Use ctrl +O when you want to locate or open a file or program.*

5. **Ctrl + P:** Control plus P prints the active document. *Always use this to locate the printer dialog box and print.*

6. **Ctrl + S:** Control plus S saves a new document or file and changes made by the user. *Going for the mouse? Please stop! Don't use the mouse. Just press Ctrl+S and everything will be saved.*

7. **Ctrl +V:** Control plus V pastes copied elements into the active area of the program in use. *Using ctrl+V in a case like this Saves the time and stress of right clicking and clicking again just to paste.*

8. **Ctrl + W:** Control plus W is used to close the page you are working on when you want to leave the work environment.

> *"There is a way Peace does this without using the mouse. Oh my God, why didn't I learn it then?"* Don't worry, I have the answer, Peace presses Ctrl+W to close active windows.

9. **Ctrl + X:** Control plus X cuts elements (making the elements to disappear from their original place). The difference between cutting and deleting elements is that in Cutting, what was cut doesn't get lost permanently but prepares itself so that it can be pasted in another location selected by the user.

> *Use ctrl+x when you think* **"this shouldn't be here and I can't stand the stress of retyping or redesigning it in the rightful place it belongs".**

10. **Ctrl + Y:** Control plus Y redoes an undone action.

> *Ctrl+Z brought back what you didn't need? Press Ctrl+ Y to remove it again.*

11. **Ctrl + Z:** Control plus Z undoes actions.

Can't find what you typed now or a picture you inserted, it suddenly disappeared or you mistakenly removed it? Press Ctrl+Z to bring it back.

12. **Alt + F4:** Alternative plus F4 closes active windows or items.

   *You don't need to move the mouse in order to close an active window, just press **Alt + F4** if you are done or don't want somebody who is coming to see what you are doing.*

13. **Ctrl + F6:** Control plus F6 Navigates between open windows, making it possible for a user to see what is happening in windows that are active.
   Are you working in Microsoft Word and want to find out if the other active window where your browser is loading a page is still progressing? Use Ctrl + F6.

14. **F1:** This displays the help window.

   *Is your computer malfunctioning? Use **F1** to find help when you don't know what next to do.*

15. **F12:** This enables user to make changes to an already saved document.

F12 is the shortcut to use when you want to change the format in which you saved your existing document, password it, change its name, change the file location or destination, or make other changes to it. It will save your time.

CHAPTER 3.

Keyboard Shortcuts In Word 2016.

Definition of Program: Microsoft Word is a word processing program designed in 1983 by Microsoft Corporation. It allows users to create and modify simple and sophisticated documents.

The following list contains keyboard shortcuts that will boost your productivity in Microsoft Word.

Frequently Used Shortcuts.

This table shows the most frequently used shortcuts in Microsoft Word.

TASK	SHORTCUT
Go to "Tell me what you want to do"	ALT+Q
Open	CTRL+O
Save	CTRL+S
Close	CTRL+W
Cut	CTRL+X
Copy	CTRL+C
Paste	CTRL+V

Select all	CTRL+A
Bold	CTRL+B
Italic	CTRL+I
Underline	CTRL+U
Decrease font size 1 point	CTRL+[
Increase font size 1 point	CTRL+]
Center text	CTRL+E
Left align text	CTRL+L
Right align text	CTRL+R
Cancel	Esc
Undo	CTRL+Z
Re-do	CTRL+Y
Zoom	ALT+W, Q, then tab in Zoom dialog box to the value you want.

Navigate The Ribbon With Only The Keyboard.

The ribbon is the strip at the top of Word, organized by tabs. Each tab displays a different ribbon. Ribbons are made up of groups, and each group includes one or more commands. Every command in Word can be accessed by using shortcut.

Note: Add-ins and other programs may add new tabs to the ribbon and may provide access keys for those tabs.

There are two ways to navigate the tabs in the ribbon:

- To go to the ribbon, press Alt, and then, to move between tabs, use the Right Arrow and Left Arrow keys.
- To go directly to a specific tab on the ribbon, use one of the access keys

TASK	SHORTCUT
To use Backstage view, open the **File** page.	ALT+F
To use themes, colors, and effects, such as page borders, open the **Design** tab.	ALT+G
To use common formatting commands, paragraph styles, or to use the Find tool. open **Home** tab.	ALT+H
To manage Mail Merge tasks, or to work with envelopes and labels, open **Mailings** tab.	ALT+M
To insert tables, pictures and shapes, headers, or text boxes, open **Insert** tab.	ALT+N
To work with page margins, page orientation, indentation, and spacing, open **Layout** tab.	ALT+P
To type a search term for Help content, open "Tell me" box on ribbon.	ALT+Q, then enter the search term
To use Spell Check, set proofing languages, or to track and review changes to your document, open the **Review** tab.	ALT+R
To add a table of contents,	ALT+S

footnotes, or a table of citations, open the **References** tab.	
To choose a document view or mode, such as Read Mode or Outline view, open the **View** tab. You can also set Zoom magnification and manage multiple windows of documents.	ALT+W

Use commands on a ribbon with the keyboard

- To move to the list of ribbon tabs, press Alt; to go directly to a tab, press a keyboard shortcut.
- To move into the ribbon, press the Down Arrow key. (JAWS refers to this action as a move to the lower ribbon.)
- To move between commands, press the Tab key or Shift+Tab.
- To move in the group that's currently selected, press the Down Arrow key.
- To move between groups on a ribbon, press Ctrl+Right Arrow or Ctrl+Left Arrow.
- Controls on the ribbon are activated in different ways, depending upon the type of control:
  - If the selected command is a button, to activate it, press SPACEBAR or ENTER.
  - If the selected command is a split button (that is, a button that opens a menu of additional options), to activate it, press Alt+Down Arrow. Tab through the options. To select the current option, press SPACEBAR or ENTER.

- If the selected command is a list (such as the Font list), to open the list, press the Down Arrow key. Then, to move between items, use the Up Arrow or Down Arrow key.
- If the selected command is a gallery, to select the command, press SPACEBAR or ENTER. Then, tab through the items.

Tip: In galleries with more than one row of items, the Tab key moves from the beginning to the end of the current row and, when it reaches the end of the row, it moves to the beginning of the next one. Pressing the Right Arrow key at the end of the current row moves back to the beginning of the current row.

Use access keys when you can see the KeyTips

To use access keys:

1. Press ALT.
2. Press the letter shown in the square KeyTip that appears over the ribbon command that you want to use.

Depending on which letter you press, you may be shown additional KeyTips. For example, if you press ALT+F, the Office Backstage opens on the Info page which has a different set of KeyTips. If you then press ALT again, KeyTips for navigating on this page appear.

Change The Keyboard Focus By Using The Keyboard Without Using The Mouse

The following table lists some ways to move the keyboard focus when using only the keyboard.

TASK	SHORTCUT
Select the active tab of the ribbon and activate the access keys.	ALT or F10. Use access keys or arrow keys to move to a different tab.
Move the focus to commands on the ribbon.	TAB or SHIFT+TAB
Move the focus to each command on the ribbon, forward or backward, respectively.	TAB or SHIFT+TAB
Move down, up, left, or right, respectively, among the items on the ribbon.	DOWN ARROW, UP ARROW, LEFT ARROW, or RIGHT ARROW
Expand or collapse the ribbon.	CTRL+F1
Display the shortcut menu for a selected item.	SHIFT+F10
Move the focus to a different pane of the window, such as the Format Picture pane, the Grammar pane, or the Selection pane.	F6
Activate a selected	SPACEBAR or

command or control on the ribbon.	ENTER
Open a selected menu or gallery on the ribbon.	SPACEBAR or ENTER
Finish modifying a value in a control on the ribbon, and move focus back to the document.	ENTER

Keyboard Shortcuts For SmartArt Graphics.

Insert a SmartArt graphic in an Office document

1. In the Microsoft Office program where you want to insert the graphic, press Alt, then N, and then M to open the **SmartArt Graphic** dialog box.
2. Press Up Arrow or Down Arrow to select the type of graphic that you want.
3. Press Tab to move to the Layout task pane.
4. Press the arrow keys to select the layout that you want.
5. Press Enter to insert the selected layout.

Work With Shapes In A SmartArt Graphic

TASK	SHORTCUT
Select the next element in a SmartArt graphic.	Tab
Select the previous element in a SmartArt graphic.	Shift+Tab
Select all shapes.	Ctrl +A

Remove focus from the selected shape.	Esc
Nudge the selected shape up.	Up Arrow
Nudge the selected shape down.	Down Arrow
Nudge the selected shape left.	Left Arrow
Nudge the selected shape right.	Right Arrow
Edit text in the selected shape.	Enter or F2, Esc to exit shape
Delete the selected shape.	Delete or Backspace
Cut the selected shape.	Ctrl+X or Shift+Delete
Copy the selected shape.	Ctrl+C
Paste the contents of the Clipboard.	Ctrl+V
Undo the last action.	Ctrl+Z

Move And Resize Shapes In A SmartArt Graphic

TASK	SHORTCUT
Enlarge the selected shape horizontally.	Shift+Right Arrow
Reduce the selected shape horizontally.	Shift+Left Arrow
Enlarge the selected shape vertically.	Shift+Up Arrow
Reduce the selected shape vertically.	Shift+Down Arrow
Rotate the selected shape to the right.	Alt+Right Arrow

Rotate the selected shape to the left.	Alt+Left Arrow

Notes:

- To apply more precise adjustments to shapes, press the Ctrl key in addition to any of the above keyboard shortcuts.
- These keyboard shortcuts apply to multiple selections as if you selected each item individually.

Work With Text In A SmartArt Graphic

TASK	SHORTCUT
Move one character to the left.	Left Arrow
Move one character to the right.	Right Arrow
Move up one line.	Up Arrow
Move down one line.	Down Arrow
Move one word to the left.	Ctrl+Left Arrow
Move one word to the right.	Ctrl+Right Arrow
Move one paragraph up.	Ctrl+Up Arrow
Move one paragraph down.	Ctrl+Down Arrow
Move to the end of a line.	End
Move to the beginning of a line.	Home
Move to the end of a text box.	Ctrl+End
Move to the beginning of a text box.	Ctrl+Home
Cut selected text.	Ctrl+X
Copy selected text.	Ctrl+C

Paste selected text.	Ctrl+V
Move the selected text up.	Alt+Shift+Up Arrow
Move the selected text down.	Alt+Shift+Down Arrow
Undo the last action.	Ctrl+Z
Delete one character to the left.	Backspace
Delete one word to the left.	Ctrl+Backspace
Delete one character to the right.	Delete
Delete one word to the right.	Ctrl+Delete
Promote the selected text.	Alt+Shift+Left Arrow
Demote the selected text.	Alt+Shift+Right Arrow
Check the spelling (not available in Word).	F7

Apply Character Formatting

TASK	SHORTCUT
Open the **Font** dialog box.	Ctrl+Shift+F or Ctrl+Shift+P
Increase the font size of the selected text.	Ctrl+Shift+>
Decrease the font size of the selected text.	Ctrl+Shift+<
Switch the case of selected text (lower case, Title Case, UPPER CASE).	Shift+F3
Apply bold formatting to the selected text.	Ctrl+B
Apply an underline to the	Ctrl+U

selected text.	
Apply italic formatting to the selected text.	Ctrl+I
Apply subscript formatting to the selected text.	Ctrl+Equal Sign
Apply superscript formatting to the selected text.	Ctrl+Shift+Plus Sign
Adjust the superscript/subscript offset up.	Ctrl+Alt+Shift+>
Adjust the superscript/subscript offset down.	Ctrl+Alt+Shift+<
Remove all character formatting from the selected text.	Shift+Ctrl+Spacebar

Copy Text Formatting

TASK	SHORTCUT
Copy formatting from the selected text.	Shift+Ctrl+C
Paste formatting to the selected text.	Shift+Ctrl+V

Apply Paragraph Formatting

TASK	SHORTCUT
Center a paragraph.	Ctrl+E
Justify a paragraph.	Ctrl+J
Left align a paragraph.	Ctrl+L
Right align a	Ctrl+R

paragraph.	
Demote a bullet point.	Tab or Alt+Shift+Right Arrow
Promote a bullet point.	Shift+Tab or Alt+Shift+Left Arrow

Use The Text Pane

TASK	SHORTCUT
Merge two lines of text.	Delete at the end of the first line of text
Display the shortcut menu.	Shift+F10
Switch between the **Text** pane and the drawing canvas.	Ctrl+Shift+F2
Close the **Text** pane.	Alt+F4
Switch the focus from the **Text** pane to the border of the SmartArt graphic.	Esc
Open the SmartArt graphics Help topic. (Your pointer should be in the Text pane.)	Ctrl +Shift+F1

□

Use The Keyboard To Work With The Ribbon.

Do tasks quickly without using the mouse by pressing a few keys—no matter where you are in an Office program. You can get to every command on the ribbon by using an access key—usually by pressing two to four keys.

1. Press and release the ALT key.

You see the little boxes called KeyTips over each command available in the current view.

2. Press the letter shown in the KeyTip over the command you want to use.
3. Depending on which letter you pressed, you might see additional KeyTips. For example, if the **Home** tab is active and you pressed N, the **Insert** tab is displayed, along with the KeyTips for the groups in that tab.
4. Continue pressing letters until you press the letter of the specific command you want to use.

Tip: To cancel the action you're taking and hide the KeyTips, press and release the ALT key.

Change the keyboard focus without using the mouse

Another way to use the keyboard to work with the ribbon is to move the focus among the tabs and commands until you find the feature you want to use. The following shows some ways to move the keyboard focus without using the mouse.

TASK	SHORTCUT
Select the active tab and show the access keys.	ALT or F10. Press either of these keys again to move back to the Office file and cancel the access keys.
Move to another tab.	ALT or F10 to select the active tab, and then

	LEFT ARROW or RIGHT ARROW.
Move to another Group on the active tab.	ALT or F10 to select the active tab, and then CTRL+RIGHT ARROW or LEFT ARROW to move between groups.
Minimize (collapse) or restore the ribbon.	CTRL+F1
Display the shortcut menu for the selected item.	SHIFT+F10
Move the focus to select the active tab, your Office file, task pane, or status bar.	F6
Move the focus to each command in the ribbon, forward or backward.	ALT or F10, and then TAB or SHIFT+TAB
Move down, up, left, or right among the items in the ribbon.	DOWN ARROW, UP ARROW, LEFT ARROW, or RIGHT ARROW
Go to the selected command or control in the ribbon.	SPACE BAR or ENTER
Open the selected menu or gallery in the ribbon.	SPACE BAR or ENTER
Go to a command or option in the ribbon so you can change it.	ENTER
Finish changing the value of a command or option in the ribbon, and move	ENTER

focus back to the Office file.	
Get help on the selected command or control in the ribbon. (If no Help article is associated with the selected command, the Help table of contents for that program is shown instead.)	F1

Keyboard Shortcut Reference For Microsoft Word.

Create and edit documents

Create, view, and save documents

TASK	SHORTCUT
Create a new document.	CTRL+N
Open a document.	CTRL+O
Close a document.	CTRL+W
Split the document window.	ALT+CTRL+S
Remove the document window split.	ALT+SHIFT+C or ALT+CTRL+S
Save a document.	CTRL+S

Work with Web content

TASK	SHORTCUT
Insert a hyperlink.	CTRL+K

Go back one page.	ALT+LEFT ARROW
Go forward one page.	ALT+RIGHT ARROW
Refresh.	F9

Print and preview documents

TASK	SHORTCUT
Print a document.	CTRL+P
Switch to print preview.	ALT+CTRL+I
Move around the preview page when zoomed in.	Arrow keys
Move by one preview page when zoomed out.	PAGE UP or PAGE DOWN
Move to the first preview page when zoomed out.	CTRL+HOME
Move to the last preview page when zoomed out.	CTRL+END

Check spelling and review changes in a document

TASK	SHORTCUT
Insert a comment (in the Revision task pane).	ALT+R, C
Turn change tracking on or off.	CTRL+SHIFT+E
Close the Reviewing Pane if it is open.	ALT+SHIFT+C
Select Review tab on ribbon.	ALT+R, then DOWN ARROW to move to commands on this tab.
Select Spelling & Grammar	ALT+R, S

Find, replace, and go to specific items in the document

TASK	SHORTCUT
Open the search box in the **Navigation** task pane.	CTRL+F
Replace text, specific formatting, and special items.	CTRL+H
Go to a page, bookmark, footnote, table, comment, graphic, or other location.	CTRL+G
Switch between the last four places that you have edited.	ALT+CTRL+Z

Move around in a document using the keyboard

TASK	SHORTCUT
One character to the left	LEFT ARROW
One character to the right	RIGHT ARROW
One word to the left	CTRL+LEFT ARROW
One word to the right	CTRL+RIGHT ARROW
One paragraph up	CTRL+UP ARROW
One paragraph down	CTRL+DOWN ARROW
One cell to the left (in a table)	SHIFT+TAB
One cell to the right (in a table)	TAB
Up one line	UP ARROW
Down one line	DOWN ARROW
To the end of a line	END
To the beginning of a line	HOME

To the top of the window	ALT+CTRL+PAGE UP
To the end of the window	ALT+CTRL+PAGE DOWN
Up one screen (scrolling)	PAGE UP
Down one screen (scrolling)	PAGE DOWN
To the top of the next page	CTRL+PAGE DOWN
To the top of the previous page	CTRL+PAGE UP
To the end of a document	CTRL+END
To the beginning of a document	CTRL+HOME
To a previous revision	SHIFT+F5
After opening a document, to the location you were working in when the document was last closed	SHIFT+F5

Insert or mark Table of Contents, footnotes, and citations

TASK	SHORTCUT
Mark a table of contents entry.	ALT+SHIFT+O
Mark a table of authorities entry (citation).	ALT+SHIFT+I
Mark an index entry.	ALT+SHIFT+X
Insert a footnote.	ALT+CTRL+F
Insert an endnote.	ALT+CTRL+D
Go to next footnote (in Word 2016).	ALT+SHIFT+>
Go to previous footnote (in Word 2016).	ALT+SHIFT+<

Go to "Tell me what you want to do" and Smart Lookup (in Word 2016).	ALT+Q

Work with documents in different views

Word offers several different views of a document. Each view makes it easier to do certain tasks. For example, Read Mode enables you to present two pages of the document side by side, and to use an arrow navigation to move to the next page.

Switch to another view of the document

TASK	SHORTCUT
Switch to Read Mode view	ALT+W, F
Switch to Print Layout view.	ALT+CTRL+P
Switch to Outline view.	ALT+CTRL+O
Switch to Draft view.	ALT+CTRL+N

Work with headings in Outline view

These shortcuts only apply if a document is in Outline view.

TASK	SHORTCUT
Promote a paragraph.	ALT+SHIFT+LEFT ARROW
Demote a paragraph.	ALT+SHIFT+RIGHT ARROW
Demote to body text.	CTRL+SHIFT+N
Move selected paragraphs up.	ALT+SHIFT+UP ARROW

Move selected paragraphs down.	ALT+SHIFT+DOWN ARROW
Expand text under a heading.	ALT+SHIFT+PLUS SIGN
Collapse text under a heading.	ALT+SHIFT+MINUS SIGN
Expand or collapse all text or headings.	ALT+SHIFT+A
Hide or display character formatting.	The slash (/) key on the numeric keypad
Show the first line of text or all text.	ALT+SHIFT+L
Show all headings with the Heading 1 style.	ALT+SHIFT+1
Show all headings up to Heading n.	ALT+SHIFT+n
Insert a tab character.	CTRL+TAB

Navigate in Read Mode view

TASK	SHORTCUT
Go to beginning of document.	HOME
Go to end of document.	END
Go to page n.	n (n is the page number you want to go to), ENTER
Exit Read mode.	ESC

Edit and move text and graphics

Select text and graphics

Select text by holding down SHIFT and using the arrow keys to move the cursor

Extend a selection

TASK	SHORTCUT
Turn extend mode on.	F8
Select the nearest character.	F8, and then press LEFT ARROW or RIGHT ARROW
Increase the size of a selection.	F8 (press once to select a word, twice to select a sentence, and so on)
Reduce the size of a selection.	SHIFT+F8
Turn extend mode off.	ESC
Extend a selection one character to the right.	SHIFT+RIGHT ARROW
Extend a selection one character to the left.	SHIFT+LEFT ARROW
Extend a selection to the end of a word.	CTRL+SHIFT+RIGHT ARROW
Extend a selection to the beginning of a word.	CTRL+SHIFT+LEFT ARROW

Extend a selection to the end of a line.	SHIFT+END
Extend a selection to the beginning of a line.	SHIFT+HOME
Extend a selection one line down.	SHIFT+DOWN ARROW
Extend a selection one line up.	SHIFT+UP ARROW
Extend a selection to the end of a paragraph.	CTRL+SHIFT+DOWN ARROW
Extend a selection to the beginning of a paragraph.	CTRL+SHIFT+UP ARROW
Extend a selection one screen down.	SHIFT+PAGE DOWN
Extend a selection one screen up.	SHIFT+PAGE UP
Extend a selection to the beginning of a document.	CTRL+SHIFT+HOME
Extend a selection to the	CTRL+SHIFT+END

end of a document.	
Extend a selection to the end of a window.	ALT+CTRL+SHIFT+PAGE DOWN
Extend a selection to include the entire document.	CTRL+A
Select a vertical block of text.	CTRL+SHIFT+F8, and then use the arrow keys; press ESC to cancel selection mode
Extend a selection to a specific location in a document.	F8+arrow keys; press ESC to cancel selection mode

Delete text and graphics

TASK	SHORTCUT
Delete one character to the left.	BACKSPACE
Delete one word to the left.	CTRL+BACKSPACE
Delete one character to the right.	DELETE
Delete one word to the right.	CTRL+DELETE
Cut selected text to the Office Clipboard.	CTRL+X
Undo the last action.	CTRL+Z
Cut to the Spike. (Spike is a feature that allows you to	CTRL+F3

collect groups of text from different locations and paste them in another location).	

Copy and move text and graphics

TASK	SHORTCUT
Open the Office Clipboard	Press ALT+H to move to the **Home** tab, and then press F,O.
Copy selected text or graphics to the Office Clipboard.	CTRL+C
Cut selected text or graphics to the Office Clipboard.	CTRL+X
Paste the most recent addition or pasted item from the Office Clipboard.	CTRL+V
Move text or graphics once.	F2 (then move the cursor and press ENTER)
Copy text or graphics once.	SHIFT+F2 (then move the cursor and press ENTER)
When text or an object is selected, open the **Create New Building Block** dialog box.	ALT+F3
When the building block — for example, a SmartArt graphic — is selected, display the	SHIFT+F10

shortcut menu that is associated with it.	
Cut to the Spike.	CTRL+F3
Paste the Spike contents.	CTRL+SHIFT+F3
Copy the header or footer used in the previous section of the document.	ALT+SHIFT+R

Edit and navigate tables

Select text and graphics in a table

TASK	SHORTCUT
Select the next cell's contents.	TAB
Select the preceding cell's contents.	SHIFT+TAB
Extend a selection to adjacent cells.	Hold down SHIFT and press an arrow key repeatedly
Select a column.	Use the arrow keys to move to the column's top or bottom cell, and then do one of the following: • Press SHIFT+ALT+PAGE DOWN to select the column from top to bottom. • Press SHIFT+ALT+PAGE UP to select the column from

	bottom to top.
Select an entire row	Use arrow keys to move to end of the row, either the first cell (leftmost) in the row or to the last cell (rightmost) in the row. • From the first cell in the row, press SHIFT+ALT+END to select the row from left to right. • From the last cell in the row, press SHIFT+ALT+HOME to select the row from right to left.
Extend a selection (or block).	CTRL+SHIFT+F8, and then use the arrow keys; press ESC to cancel selection mode
Select an entire table.	ALT+5 on the numeric keypad (with NUM LOCK off)

Move around in a table

TASK	SHORTCUT
To the next cell in a row	TAB
To the previous cell in a row	SHIFT+TAB
To the first cell in a row	ALT+HOME
To the last cell in a row	ALT+END
To the first cell in a column	ALT+PAGE UP

To the last cell in a column	ALT+PAGE DOWN
To the previous row	UP ARROW
To the next row	DOWN ARROW
Row up	ALT+SHIFT+UP ARROW
Row down	ALT+SHIFT+DOWN ARROW

Insert paragraphs and tab characters in a table

TASK	SHORTCUT
New paragraphs in a cell	ENTER
Tab characters in a cell	CTRL+TAB

Format characters and paragraphs

Format characters

TASK	SHORTCUT
Open the **Font** dialog box to change the formatting of characters.	CTRL+D
Change the case of letters.	SHIFT+F3
Format all letters as capitals.	CTRL+SHIFT+A
Apply bold formatting.	CTRL+B
Apply an underline.	CTRL+U
Underline words but not spaces.	CTRL+SHIFT+W
Double-underline text.	CTRL+SHIFT+D
Apply hidden text formatting.	CTRL+SHIFT+H
Apply italic formatting.	CTRL+I

Format letters as small capitals.	CTRL+SHIFT+K
Apply subscript formatting (automatic spacing).	CTRL+EQUAL SIGN
Apply superscript formatting (automatic spacing).	CTRL+SHIFT+PLUS SIGN
Remove manual character formatting.	CTRL+SPACEBAR
Change the selection to the Symbol font.	CTRL+SHIFT+Q

Change or re-size the font

TASK	SHORTCUT
Open the **Font** dialog box to change the font.	CTRL+SHIFT+F
Increase the font size.	CTRL+SHIFT+>
Decrease the font size.	CTRL+SHIFT+<
Increase the font size by 1 point.	CTRL+]
Decrease the font size by 1 point.	CTRL+[

Copy formatting

TASK	SHORTCUT
Copy formatting from text.	CTRL+SHIFT+C
Apply copied formatting to text.	CTRL+SHIFT+V

Change paragraph alignment

TASK	SHORTCUT
Switch a paragraph between centered and left-aligned.	CTRL+E

Switch a paragraph between justified and left-aligned.	CTRL+J
Switch a paragraph between right-aligned and left-aligned.	CTRL+R
Left align a paragraph.	CTRL+L
Indent a paragraph from the left.	CTRL+M
Remove a paragraph indent from the left.	CTRL+SHIFT+M
Create a hanging indent.	CTRL+T
Reduce a hanging indent.	CTRL+SHIFT+T
Remove paragraph formatting.	CTRL+Q

Copy and review text formats

TASK	SHORTCUT
Display nonprinting characters.	CTRL+SHIFT+* (asterisk on numeric keypad does not work)
Review text formatting.	SHIFT+F1 (then click the text with the formatting you want to review)
Copy formats.	CTRL+SHIFT+C
Paste formats.	CTRL+SHIFT+V

Set line spacing

TASK	SHORTCUT
Single-space lines.	CTRL+1
Double-space lines.	CTRL+2
Set 1.5-line spacing.	CTRL+5
Add or remove one line space preceding a paragraph.	CTRL+0 (zero)

Apply Styles to paragraphs

TASK	SHORTCUT
Open **Apply Styles** task pane.	CTRL+SHIFT+S
Open **Styles** task pane.	ALT+CTRL+SHIFT+S
Start AutoFormat.	ALT+CTRL+K
Apply the Normal style.	CTRL+SHIFT+N
Apply the Heading 1 style.	ALT+CTRL+1
Apply the Heading 2 style.	ALT+CTRL+2
Apply the Heading 3 style.	ALT+CTRL+3

To close the Styles task pane

1. If the **Styles** task pane is not selected, press F6 to select it.
2. Press CTRL+SPACEBAR.
3. Use the arrow keys to select **Close**, and then press ENTER.

Insert special characters

TASK	SHORTCUT
A field	CTRL+F9
A line break	SHIFT+ENTER
A page break	CTRL+ENTER
A column break	CTRL+SHIFT+ENTER
An em dash	ALT+CTRL+MINUS SIGN (on the numeric keypad)
An en dash	CTRL+MINUS SIGN (on the numeric keypad)
An optional	CTRL+HYPHEN

hyphen	
A nonbreaking hyphen	CTRL+SHIFT+HYPHEN
A nonbreaking space	CTRL+SHIFT+SPACEBAR
The copyright symbol	ALT+CTRL+C
The registered trademark symbol	ALT+CTRL+R
The trademark symbol	ALT+CTRL+T
An ellipsis	ALT+CTRL+PERIOD
A single opening quotation mark	CTRL+`(single quotation mark), `(single quotation mark)
A single closing quotation mark	CTRL+' (single quotation mark), ' (single quotation mark)
Double opening quotation marks	CTRL+` (single quotation mark), SHIFT+' (single quotation mark)
Double closing quotation marks	CTRL+' (single quotation mark), SHIFT+' (single quotation mark)
An AutoText entry	ENTER (after you type the first few characters of the AutoText entry name and when the ScreenTip appears)

Insert characters by using character codes

TASK	SHORTCUT
Insert the Unicode character for the specified Unicode (hexadecimal) character code. For example, to insert the euro currency symbol (€), type **20AC**, and then hold down ALT and press X.	The character code, ALT+X
Find out the Unicode character code for the selected character	ALT+X
Insert the ANSI character for the specified ANSI (decimal) character code. For example, to insert the euro currency symbol, hold down ALT and press 0128 on the numeric keypad.	ALT+the character code (on the numeric keypad)

Insert and edit objects

Insert an object

1. Press ALT, N, J, and then J to open the **Object** dialog box.
2. Do one of the following.
    - Press DOWN ARROW to select an object type, and then press ENTER to create an object.
    - Press CTRL+TAB to switch to the **Create from File** tab, press TAB, and then type the file name of the object that you want to insert or browse to the file.

Edit an object

1. With the cursor positioned to the left of the object in your document, select the object by pressing SHIFT+RIGHT ARROW.
2. Press SHIFT+F10.
3. Press the TAB key to get to **Object name**, press ENTER, and then press ENTER again.

Insert SmartArt graphics

1. Press and release ALT, N, and then M to select **SmartArt**.
2. Press the arrow keys to select the type of graphic that you want.
3. Press TAB, and then press the arrow keys to select the graphic that you want to insert.
4. Press ENTER.

Insert WordArt

1. Press and release ALT, N, and then W to select **WordArt**.
2. Press the arrow keys to select the WordArt style that you want, and then press ENTER.
3. Type the text that you want.
4. Press ESC to select the WordArt object, and then use the arrow keys to move the object.
5. Press ESC again to return to return to the document.

Mail merge and fields

Note: You must press ALT+M, or click **Mailings**, to use these keyboard shortcuts.

Perform a mail merge

TASK	SHORTCUT
Preview a mail merge.	ALT+SHIFT+K
Merge a document.	ALT+SHIFT+N
Print the merged document.	ALT+SHIFT+M
Edit a mail-merge data document.	ALT+SHIFT+E
Insert a merge field.	ALT+SHIFT+F

Work with fields

TASK	SHORTCUT
Insert a DATE field.	ALT+SHIFT+D
Insert a LISTNUM field.	ALT+CTRL+L
Insert a PAGE field.	ALT+SHIFT+P
Insert a TIME field.	ALT+SHIFT+T
Insert an empty field.	CTRL+F9
Update linked information in a Microsoft Word source document.	CTRL+SHIFT+F7
Update selected fields.	F9
Unlink a field.	CTRL+SHIFT+F9
Switch between a selected field code and its result.	SHIFT+F9
Switch between all field codes and their results.	ALT+F9
Run GOTOBUTTON or MACROBUTTON from the field that displays the field results.	ALT+SHIFT+F9

Go to the next field.	F11
Go to the previous field.	SHIFT+F11
Lock a field.	CTRL+F11
Unlock a field.	CTRL+SHIFT+F11

Language Bar

Set proofing language

Every document has a default language, typically the same default language as your computer's operating system. But If your document also contains words or phrases in a different language, it's a good idea to set the proofing language for those words. This not only makes it possible to check spelling and grammar for those phrases, it makes it possible for assistive technologies like screen readers to handle them.

TASK	SHORTCUT
Open the **Set Proofing Language** dialog box	ALT+R, U, L
Review list of proofing languages	DOWN ARROW
Set default languages	ALT+R, L

Turn on East Asian Input Method Editors

TASK	SHORTCUT
Turn Japanese Input Method Editor (IME) on 101 keyboard on or off.	ALT+~
Turn Korean Input Method Editor (IME) on 101 keyboard	Right ALT

on or off.	
Turn Chinese Input Method Editor (IME) on 101 keyboard on or off.	CTRL+SPACEBAR

Function Key Reference.

Function keys

TASK	SHORTCUT
Get Help or visit Office.com.	F1
Move text or graphics.	F2
Repeat the last action.	F4
Choose the **Go To** command (**Home** tab).	F5
Go to the next pane or frame.	F6
Choose the **Spelling** command (**Review** tab).	F7
Extend a selection.	F8
Update the selected fields.	F9
Show KeyTips.	F10
Go to the next field.	F11
Choose the **Save As** command.	F12

SHIFT+Function Keys

TASK	SHORTCUT
Start context-sensitive Help or reveal formatting.	SHIFT+F1
Copy text.	SHIFT+F2
Change the case of letters.	SHIFT+F3
Repeat a **Find** or **Go To** action.	SHIFT+F4
Move to the last change.	SHIFT+F5

Go to the previous pane or frame (after pressing F6).	SHIFT+F6
Choose the **Thesaurus** command (**Review** tab, **Proofing** group).	SHIFT+F7
Reduce the size of a selection.	SHIFT+F8
Switch between a field code and its result.	SHIFT+F9
Display a shortcut menu.	SHIFT+F10
Go to the previous field.	SHIFT+F11
Choose the **Save** command.	SHIFT+F12

CTRL+Function Keys

TASK	SHORTCUT
Expand or collapse the ribbon.	CTRL+F1
Choose the **Print Preview** command.	CTRL+F2
Cut to the Spike.	CTRL+F3
Close the window.	CTRL+F4
Go to the next window.	CTRL+F6
Insert an empty field.	CTRL+F9
Maximize the document window.	CTRL+F10
Lock a field.	CTRL+F11
Choose the **Open** command.	CTRL+F12

CTRL+SHIFT+Function Keys

TASK	SHORTCUT
Insert the contents of the Spike.	CTRL+SHIFT+F3
Edit a bookmark.	CTRL+SHIFT+F5
Go to the previous window.	CTRL+SHIFT+F6

Update linked information in a Word source document.	CTRL+SHIFT+F7
Extend a selection or block.	CTRL+SHIFT+F8, and then press an arrow key
Unlink a field.	CTRL+SHIFT+F9
Unlock a field.	CTRL+SHIFT+F11
Choose the **Print** command.	CTRL+SHIFT+F12

ALT+Function keys

TASK	SHORTCUT
Go to the next field.	ALT+F1
Create a new **Building Block**.	ALT+F3
Exit Word.	ALT+F4
Restore the program window size.	ALT+F5
Move from an open dialog box back to the document, for dialog boxes that support this behavior.	ALT+F6
Find the next misspelling or grammatical error.	ALT+F7
Run a macro.	ALT+F8
Switch between all field codes and their results.	ALT+F9
Display the **Selection** task pane.	ALT+F10
Display Microsoft Visual Basic code.	ALT+F11

ALT+SHIFT+Function keys

TASK	SHORTCUT
Go to the previous field.	ALT+SHIFT+F1
Choose the **Save** command.	ALT+SHIFT+F2

Run GOTOBUTTON or MACROBUTTON from the field that displays the field results.	ALT+SHIFT+F9
Display a menu or message for an available action.	ALT+SHIFT+F10
Choose **Table of Contents** button in the Table of Contents container when the container is active.	ALT+SHIFT+F12

CTRL+ALT+Function keys

TASK	SHORTCUT
Display Microsoft System Information.	CTRL+ALT+F1
Choose the **Open** command.	CTRL+ALT+F2

☐

Customer's Page.

This page is for customers who enjoyed Microsoft Word 2016 Keyboard Shortcuts For Windows.

Dearly beloved customer, please leave a review behind if you enjoyed this book or found it helpful. It will be highly appreciated, thank you.

Other Books By This Publisher.

S/N	Title	Series
Series A: Limits Breaking Quotes.		
1	Discover Your Key Christian Quotes	Limits Breaking Quotes
Series B: Shortcut Matters.		
1	Windows 7 Shortcuts	Shortcut Matters
2	Windows 7 Shortcuts & Tips	Shortcut Matters
3	Windows 8.1 Shortcuts	Shortcut Matters
4	Windows 10 Shortcut Keys	Shortcut Matters
5	Microsoft Office 2007 Keyboard Shortcuts For Windows.	Shortcut Matters
6	Microsoft Office 2010 Shortcuts For Windows.	Shortcut Matters
7	Microsoft Office 2013 Shortcuts For Windows.	Shortcut Matters
Series C: Teach Yourself.		
1	Teach Yourself Computer Fundamentals	Teach Yourself
Series D: For Painless Publishing		
1	Self-Publish it with CreateSpace.	For Painless Publishing
2	Where is my money? Now solved for Kindle and CreateSpace	For Painless Publishing
3	Describe it on Amazon	For Painless Publishing
4	How To Market That Book.	For Painless Publishing

www.ingramcontent.com/pod-product-compliance
Lightning Source LLC
Chambersburg PA
CBHW070856070326
40690CB00009B/1873